CLEAN AS A WHISTLE

Clean as a whistle
by Harriet Wylie

Ernest Benn
LONDON & TONBRIDGE

To my Mother and Father

First published in Great Britain 1980
Ernest Benn Limited.
25 New Street Square, London EC4A 3JA & Sovereign Way,
Tonbridge, KENT TN9 1RW.

Text and illustrations © Harriet Wylie 1980.
ISBN 0 510 00056-8
Typeset by Cold Composition Ltd., Tonbridge, Kent
Printed in Great Britain by Sackville Press Billericay Lt

CONTENTS

INTRODUCTION

I began collecting recipes for this book after a casual enquiry from a friend on how to clean ivory beads. While finding out, I came across so many other tips that I began to take a more serious interest in the whole business of cleaning. Old recipes and books came flooding in from relatives and friends and it became as big a job deciding what should be left out as choosing what should go in.

Most of the recipes are from old books, some as far back as 1810, but alas a number of the marvellous early formulae had to be omitted as they contain chemicals that are either no longer available or are highly dangerous. As far as I can tell all the ingredients in the book are readily available from chemists, grocers, hardware shops, builders' merchants or artists' shops.

All ingredients marked with an asterisk are poisonous, inflammable, caustic or toxic and must be used with care. Precautions can be found for each chemical in the Glossary.

I hope you will have fun trying some of these interesting alternatives to modern products and discovering that they really work just as well.

Carpet Soap   Dissolve 2 oz (57 grams) of yellow soap in 1 qt (1.14 litres) of boiling water, then add ½ oz (14 grams) of washing soda and three tablespoons of *ammonia. Mix together and pour into jars.

Mix two tablespoons of the mixture to 1 qt (1.14 litres) of warm water and apply to the carpet with a brush or flannel. Rub hard and rinse off with a clean cloth and water. Dry well with a cloth and air thoroughly. Do not saturate the carpet with water as it will rot the backing.

Brighten Faded Carpets   Remove dust with a vacuum cleaner. Then mix together one part white vinegar and three parts of boiling water. Wipe the carpet with the mixture, keeping the cloth fairly dry to prevent saturating the backing, then dry thoroughly and air well. Then rub the surface with warm breadcrumbs to revive the colour.

Curling Corners of Rugs   To prevent the corners of carpets curling, sew a triangular canvas pocket on the underside of each corner about two inches from the edges. Then place a triangular piece of sheet lead, which can be bought from a plumber, into each pocket.

Sliding Rugs   To prevent rugs sliding on polished floors, sew a small rectangle of thin rubber on the underside of each corner. A piece of an old hot water bottle is ideal.

Creeping Rugs   To prevent rugs creeping on carpets, sew a large mesh fish net to the underside of the rug.

Angora Rugs   See furs in Fabrics (page 60).

Synthetic Carpets   To clean, follow the manufacturer's instructions carefully. If using chemicals always test first.

Persian and These are sturdy, hard-wearing rugs that will
Turkish Rugs withstand heavy usage if cared for properly.

Remove all dust frequently, with a vacuum
cleaner. Always sweep in the direction of the
pile to prevent grit and dirt getting to the
foundation of the rug and damaging the
knotting.

If the rug is very dirty, wash it with carpet
soap (page 10) and very soft water, the best soft
water is obtained from a wooden rain water
butt. Before tackling the rug, test the soap and
water out on an unimportant area first to see if
the colours run.

If the colours are fast and washing is suitable,
clean the rug with a sponge wrung out in the
water and dab on the soap. Only clean a small
area at a time starting in one corner. Rinse this
area with clean water and pat dry. Repeat this
until the whole rug is clean, then dry and air
thoroughly. If the colours do run, abandon the
soap and water method and sponge with *petrol
or an alcohol like *methylated spirit or surgical
spirit. Test on a hidden area first.

When possible, drag oriental rugs over newly
fallen snow, first on one side, then the other.
Shake well and replace. This cleans the rugs
and freshens the colours.

Never dry clean Turkish and Persian rugs as
the chemicals will ruin the wool and badly
affect the colours.

For bad stains and repairs, consult an expert.

Storing Rugs Always roll the rugs with the pile to the inside.
Never fold them. Where possible store rugs in
moth-proof containers.

Protect valuable rugs by backing them with
felt.

Alcohol Sponge the stain with clear, warm water as soon as possible, and dry thoroughly.

Ballpoint Ink Sponge the stain with *methylated spirit or *carbon tetrachloride. Drip the solvent onto the stain and when the ink has dissolved rub with a clean cloth and more spirit.

Care must be taken with man made fibres as the spirits can dissolve them, so always do a test first on an unimportant area.

Blood Sponge the stain with cold water and pat dry with a towel. Repeat until the stain fades. Treat as soon as possible. Never use salt water on carpets as it will rot the backing.

Chocolate To remove hard chocolate trodden into carpets, scrape off the thick pieces with a blunt knife and gently rub any remaining stain with *carbon tetrachloride.

Blot up liquid chocolate, then sponge lightly with aerated (soda) water. Then sponge with clean warm water and dry thoroughly.

Cigarette Burns Rub the mark with fine sandpaper to remove the charred fibres. Then make a mild detergent solution and drip it slowly onto the stain, and rub gently with a clean cloth. Leave for five minutes, then sponge it off with a solution made of 1 oz (28 grams) of borax to 1 pt (0.57 litres) of water. Repeat if necessary, then rinse with clean water and dry well.

Or scrape the stain with a silver coin to remove the singed fibres.

Dried Gloss Paint To remove old gloss paint stains rub with *trichlorethylene.

Grease Cover the stain with bicarbonate of soda and rub it lightly into the pile. Leave for one hour to absorb the grease, then brush off carefully with a clean brush. Repeat if necessary.

Wipe persistent stains with *carbon tetrachloride, but test in an unimportant area first.

To remove dust and grease spots from carpets, vacuum clean well, then mix one teaspoon of *ammonia and one teacup of *turpentine into a bucket of warm water. Wipe the carpet with the mixture keeping the cloth fairly dry. Rinse with clean water and dry thoroughly.

Ink Spread cream of tartar on the stain and squeeze a few drops of lemon juice onto the powder. Then rub into the stain with a clean cloth and leave for only a minute. Brush off the powder with a clean brush and sponge immediately with warm water. Repeat if necessary but do not leave the lemon juice on for more than one minute.

If the stains are fresh, cover with a layer of fuller's earth mixed into a paste with water and leave to dry. Then brush off and repeat if necessary.

Or, rub the stain with sour milk and leave for a few minutes then wipe off with a clean dry cloth. Then rub with warm water and a few drops of *ammonia.

k, Milky Tea and Coffee To remove the grease drip a mild detergent solution or *carbon tetrachloride onto the stain, then sponge off with warm water and dry well.

Rain Water Sponge the stain with a cloth dipped in *methylated spirit. Repeat until the stain fades.

Rust   Add one teaspoon of equal parts cream of tartar and lemon juice to 1 pt (0.57 litres) of water and sponge onto the stain and leave for one minute. Rinse off with clean water quickly and dry well.

Soot   To remove soot from carpets, cover the stain with a thick layer of salt, and carefully sweep it up. Never wet the soot as it will only make the stain worse.

Tea and Coffee   Blot up the excess quickly and sponge with warm water, then dry well. This process should be enough if there is no milk in the tea or coffee. (See Milk page 13.)

Urine   Mop up the excess with paper tissues or an old rag, then sponge well with clean, warm water and rub dry. Repeat, taking care not to saturate the backing fibre. Make a solution of three tablespoons of white vinegar and one teaspoon of liquid detergent. Mix together well, drip it slowly onto the stain, and leave for fifteen minutes. Then rinse off with clean water and rub dry.

Wine   Soak up the excess as soon as possible and sprinkle the stain with an absorbent powder; salt, fuller's earth, powdered borax and talcum powder are all suitable. When the powder becomes sticky, carefully remove and add more clean powder.

Repeat until most of the stain has gone then apply a final layer of powder and leave for two hours. Finally brush it off. Remove the remaining stain with a mild detergent solution and rinse quickly with clean water. Rub dry and air well.

Water Flooding and leaks must be dealt with immediately. Mop up the excess quickly, and prop a stool or box under the wet area. Place a fan heater near it to circulate the air and dry it as quickly as possible. This is only suitable if the damp area is relatively small, but if the flooding is extensive, dry the carpet in the open air.

Once the carpet is dry, stains can be removed by dripping a mild detergent solution onto the area. Wipe off with a clean cloth then rinse and dry thoroughly.

Consult an expert if the stains are severe.

Polish for rquet Floors

Dissolve 2 oz (57 grams) of beeswax in ½pt (0.28 litres) *turpentine in a double pan, to make an oily mixture. Coat the floor with linseed oil then rub on the mixture. Leave for twenty four hours then polish hard.

Economical oor Polishes

Empty half a new tin of floor polish into another tin and fill up both the tins with *paraffin. Place the tins in a pan of cold water and bring to the boil, to melt the polish. Stir well, then cool. This diluted polish is just as effective.

Save all old ends of burnt candles. When a good quantity has been collected, shred them into a pan and weigh the contents. Remove any wicks, and add an equal quantity of *turpentine to the wax. Place the pan into another pan of cold water and bring to the boil, to melt the wax. Stir well, then pour the mixture into tins and cool. Warm the polish slightly before use to make polishing easier.

Economical Polish

Mix together ½ pt (0.28 litres) of *paraffin and ½ pt (0.28 litres) of white vinegar in a bottle and shake well before use. This is suitable for cleaning tiles, linoleum, marble and paint work.

Scrubbing Mixture for Floor Boards and Kitchen Tables

Mix together, 1 lb (0.45 kilograms) soft soap (see page 53), 1 lb (0.45 kilograms) fuller's earth. 1 lb (0.45 kilograms) soda and 2 qts (2.27 litres) of water, in a large pan. Bring to the boil and simmer until there is only half the quantity left. Then cool and store in jars.

Apply the mixture to the boards and scrub with a stiff brush and hot water. Always scrub in the direction of the grain of the wood. Then rinse and dry.

Coconut Matting   To clean coconut matting, beat it well to remove the dust. Then scrub it with warm salt water on both sides. If it is very dirty, use soap as well as the salt water method. In both cases rinse well with warm then cold water. Then hang outside to dry, keeping the matting as flat as possible. Do not hang it over a washing line as this will leave a permanent crease in it.

Linoleum   To clean linoleum, wipe it with a clean cloth wrung out in lukewarm water, and dry well. Then rub with a cloth dipped in a little warmed linseed oil to produce a good sheen.

To freshen old linoleum, mix one part of fresh milk with one part *turpentine. Rub the mixture onto the floor and polish with a warmed soft cloth.

Never use soap, *ammonia or soap powders on linoleum as they cause the surface to crack and the colour to fade.

Floor and Wall Tiles   Dissolve 4 oz (113 grams) of shredded coarse soap and 4 oz (113 grams) of washing soda in one gallon (4.5 litres) of hot water. Using a stiff brush scrub the tiles with the mixture then rinse and dry.

To remove cement from floor tiles, rub well with a little linseed oil on a cloth.

Rub glazed tiles with a cut lemon and leave for fifteen minutes, then polish with a soft cloth.

To clean discoloured tiles, wash with hot water and a little *paraffin.

Rub the tiles with French chalk and a damp cloth to remove brown stains.

Mix equal parts of linseed oil and *turpentine, to polish the tiles. This will prevent the glaze from cracking and will also produce a good sheen.

Stone Floors and Steps To clean weather stains off stone steps, scour with a stiff brush dipped in hot soapy water mixed with a tablespoon of *paraffin.

To remove grease stains, pour a strong solution of washing soda and boiling water onto the steps. Then cover the stains with a paste made of fuller's earth and hot water. Leave overnight and rinse. Repeat if necessary.

To prevent steps from freezing up in winter, add an aspirin and a tablespoon of *methylated spirit to the final rinsing water.

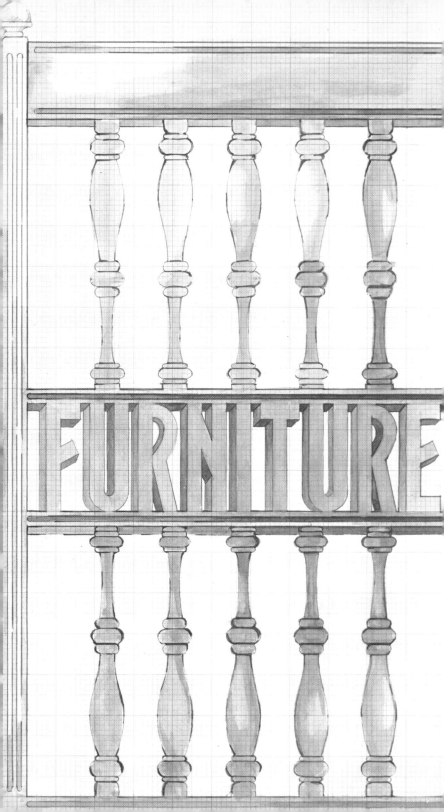

Furniture Polish

Shred 4 oz (113 grams) of beeswax into an old pan and add ½pt (0.28 litres) *turpentine. Place the pan in another pan of boiling water and heat until the wax melts. Stir thoroughly and store in jars or tins.

Liquid Polish Carved wood

Mix two parts of boiled linseed oil with one part of each of the following: *methylated spirit, *turpentine and white vinegar. Store in firmly corked bottles and shake well before use.

Furniture Cream for Polished Wood

Shred 4 oz (113 grams) of beeswax and 1 oz (28 grams) of white candle wax into a pan and add ½ pt (0.28 litres) of *turpentine. Place the pan into another pan of boiling water and heat until the wax melts, then stir thoroughly. Then dissolve ½ oz (14 grams) of shredded castile soap or pure soap flakes in a ¼ pt (0.14 litres) of boiling water and mix into a thick paste. When cool but still liquid mix the two together and beat hard to a creamy consistency, and store in jars.

A wax polished surface keeps moisture out, but it also seals it in and often prevents excessive drying which causes cracking and warping.

Polishing Hint

To make polishing large flat surfaces easier, heat a brick or an old-fashioned flat iron in the oven until hot. Wrap the hot brick in several pieces of old blanket and apply the polish to the flat side of the blanket. Then 'iron' the surface in the direction of the grain, until the whole area is covered with polish. The heat melts the wax and allows it to sink into the wood easily, and the weight of the brick eliminates arm-ache.

Dust Pump Use a bicycle pump or hair dryer to blow away dust on carved furniture, bed springs or any intricately decorated objects.

Woods To clean and feed oak, rub the surface with boiled linseed oil on a soft cloth, then polish off the excess with a soft dry leather.

Or, boil 2 pts (1.14 litres) ale with ½ oz (14 grams) of sugar and 1 oz (28 grams) of beeswax and mix thoroughly. When cool, wipe the wood with the mixture and a soft cloth. Leave to dry then polish up with a soft dry leather.

To clean polished mahogany, wipe the surface with equal parts of white vinegar and warm water, then polish with a soft cloth.

To clean walnut, rub the surface with a little *paraffin on a soft cloth, and polish with a soft dry leather.

The above recipes for woods can be used when the furniture has a natural 'patina' from many years of polishing and use. They can be used frequently with an occasional thorough polishing with beeswax and *turpentine.

Bleaching To bleach wood, scrub the surface with Milton, to remove the colour, then rinse thoroughly with water and dry quickly with a soft rag. The wood must be sealed after this process. Mix up a thin solution of plaster of Paris and water, and apply it to the whole surface and leave to dry. Then wipe off the excess with a damp cloth. The plaster of Paris will sink into the wood and seal it below the surface. Select a spirit based wood stain and brush it on to the surface evenly, then brush on a coat of white oil and polish frequently and thoroughly with beeswax polish. All stages of this process are essential to prevent warping.

Acid Baths Never use an acid bath to strip furniture, as it weakens the glues and removes all the natural oils in the wood.

Stripping ·nch Polished Furniture A lot of *methylated spirit is used in this process, so if possible work out of doors. If not, open all windows and doors to create a draught. The fumes are very heavy and can cause drowsiness and nausea in confined airless spaces. They are also highly inflammable, so make sure there are no naked flames nearby.

Wipe the surface with *methylated spirit using a nylon scouring pad, in the direction of the wood grain. Use the *methylated spirit liberally, it will dissolve the varnish and make it easy to wipe off. If the varnish is very stubborn use grade 000 wire wool. Make sure all the French polish has been removed then wipe the surface clean with a new rag and more *methylated spirit. Remove any stains (see page 25-27), and apply beeswax polish with a hot brick and blankets (see polishing hint). Polish frequently to build up a protective sheen.

turated Wood A safe way to dry out saturated woods is to immerse the object in *paraffin. It will slowly drive out the water which rises to the surface. When all the water has come out immerse the object in *petrol to drive out the *paraffin. Then take it out, and the *petrol will evaporate. When fully dry, polish in the usual way.

Dents Cover dents in wood with wet blotting paper, and press with a hot iron, repeating if necessary. The compressed wood fibres will swell to their original size. Afterwards polish as usual.

Woodworm Holes	Place the point of a penknife into the dead worm holes with the blade in the same direction as the wood grain, and push the blade in a little way to destroy the perfect circular shape of the hole. Fill the hole well with beeswax polish mixed with a little spirit based wood stain to match the colour of the wood. This is the best disguise for hiding the worm holes.
Rush and White Wicker	To clean rush, sponge with warm salt water, then rinse with hot water and dry in the sun. If the cane has yellowed, sponge with lemon juice and salt, then rinse and dry. If the cane has sagged, clean it, then saturate with hot water and dry outside.
Cane	Treat cane in the same way as rush. When dry, polish with furniture cream.
Brown Wicker	Scrub well with cold salty water and rinse in cold water and dry in the sun. When dry, brush with *paraffin and polish with a soft cloth.
Deck Chairs	Remove the canvas and wash it in soapy water with a little *ammonia. Scrub if necessary. Rinse well and dry in the open air, then press with a warm iron. Scrub the frame and replace the canvas.
Picture Frames	To clean gilt frames, mix one egg white with one teaspoon of bicarbonate of soda and sponge the surface with the mixture.

To clean gilt frames, mix one egg white with one teaspoon of bicarbonate of soda and sponge the surface with the mixture.

Or, wipe the surface with washing up liquid, then polish with a soft cloth.

To clean wooden frames, first dust then rub with a little boiled linseed oil on a soft cloth.

eneral Rules Deal with stains as soon as possible.

Alcohol To remove alcohol stains from wood, make a thick paste with pumice powder and boiled linseed oil, and rub the stain carefully, with the grain. Then wipe clean and rub with a little linseed oil and polish as usual.

Rub alcohol rings on wood with oil of camphor. If the stain is still wet, dab it with boiled linseed oil and leave for twelve hours. Rub hard before polishing as usual.

Candle Wax To remove candle grease from wood, lightly scrape off the surface wax with the back of a blunt knife, then polish with a soft leather.

Chill Marks Cloudy 'chill' marks appear on French polished furniture when exposed to extremes of temperature. To remove these marks, gently wave a lighted taper from side to side over the marks until they disappear, taking care not to scorch the varnish. Then rub over the area with a warm cloth and polish well. Keep the article in a constant temperature.

Ink and Grease To remove ink stains and grease marks from polished wood and upholstery, mix two tablespoons of white vinegar with one part of water and sponge the stains in dark woods with it. Rinse well and dry, then polish as usual.

Or, make up a 5% solution of *oxalic acid and apply it to the stains with a soft brush, a cork or a feather. When the stain has been removed, rinse with pure water and dry with clean blotting paper, then polish as usual.

Rub ink stained white wood with half a lemon dipped in salt, then rinse well with clear water. Dry thoroughly then polish as usual.

Hot Dish Marks To remove hot dish marks from polished wood, simmer 1 pt (0.57 litres) of boiled linseed oil for ten minutes and add ¼ pt (0.14 litres) of *turpentine. Apply this frequently to the stain with a soft cloth until it fades, then polish as usual.

Match Marks Rub match marks on polished or varnished wood with half a cut lemon followed by a cloth dipped in warm water. Dry quickly with a cloth, then polish as usual.

Perfume To remove perfume stains from polished wood, rub the stain lightly and quickly with a little *methylated spirit followed by plenty of boiled linseed oil. If the stain is very obstinate, leave some oil on the surface for twenty four hours, then wipe clean with a soft cloth and polish as usual.

Do not use methylated spirit on varnished surfaces as it will dissolve the varnish.

Scratches To improve scratch marks on wood, mix equal parts of boiled linseed oil and *turpentine and rub it gently into the scratch. Continue to rub until the scratch fades, then polish as usual.

White Marks Rub white stains on highly polished wood with any of the following ingredients: oil of camphor, the cut edge of a brazil nut, metal polish (page 31 silver polishes) or a mixture of cigar ash and olive oil. Then polish as usual.

Metal polish must not be used on varnished woods.

Water Rub water stains on polished wood with vaseline or boiled linseed oil and repeat frequently.

Stains on Upholstery Mix any of the following:- French chalk, talcum powder, starch and fuller's earth with water to make a thick paste, and apply it to the fabric to remove a variety of stains safely.

Remove dust and loose dirt with a vacuum cleaner.

Leather Upholstery See Leather section (pages 34-35) for leather upholstery and Morocco leather.

Fabric Stains See Fabric stains (pages 65-74) for particular stains.

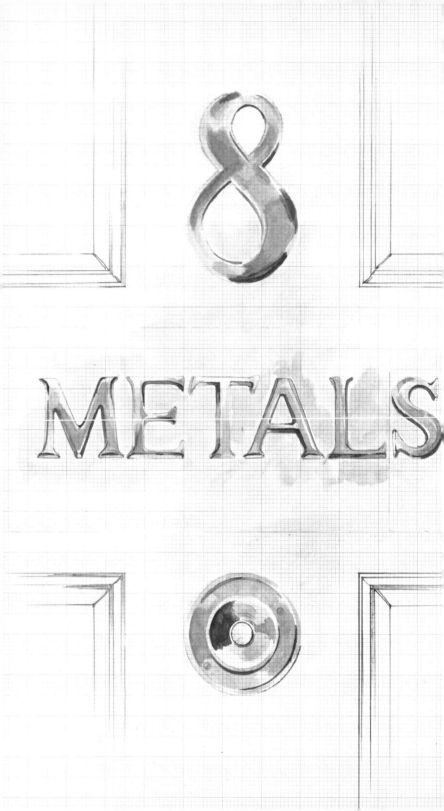

8

METALS

Aluminium To clean aluminium articles, wash with a solution of hot soapy water and a little *ammonia. Dry thoroughly and rub with dry table salt then polish with a soft cloth.

Never use washing soda on aluminium.

Brass To clean very dirty brass, boil the article in a pan of water with one tablespoon of salt and one cupful of white vinegar for several hours.

Wash engraved and Indian brass in soapy water and polish with a leather. If it is stained, rub with lemon juice and salt then wash immediately in hot soapy water. Rinse, dry and polish with a leather.

Never scour lacquered or varnished brass. Apply a paste made of lemon juice and cream of tartar, and leave on for five minutes. Then wash in warm water and dry with a soft cloth.

To remove lacquer, sponge the article with *methylated spirit. Lemon juice mixed with metal polish will help to keep the article clean longer.

Britannia Metal To clean, rub the article with a paste made of wood ash and linseed oil, wash in soapy water and dry. Then polish with a leather.

Bronze To clean bronze, dust well then rub the surface with a little warmed linseed oil, and polish with a leather.

Door Plates When cleaning door plates, cut out the exact shape and size of the door plates out of thick card. Place the template round the plate while cleaning to protect the surrounding surface.

Electroplate Wash with warm water and a little *ammonia and dry. Then rub with cigar ash and polish with a soft cloth.

Chromium Wash in warm soapy water and rinse well, then dry thoroughly. Polish with bicarbonate of soda or *methylated spirit.

To store chromium articles for long periods of time, first dismantle if necessary and coat the entire surface with a thick layer of vaseline. Make sure hinges, bolts and screws are well covered, then hang up to store. Wash off the vaseline in hot soapy water and dry thoroughly before re-using.

Copper Wash in hot soapy water and rub dry with a soft leather, then air thoroughly. To clean very dirty copper, boil the article in a pan of water with salt and white vinegar for several hours.

If tarnished, rub with a mixture of salt and white vinegar or half a lemon dipped in salt. Rinse quickly and wash in hot soapy water. Then rinse again and dry well.

If the article is caked with grime and smoke, or corroded in areas, soak in a weak solution of ammonia and cold water and gently rub with wire wool (Grade 000). Dry quickly and polish with a paste made from wood ash and *methylated spirit.

Gold Wash plain gold articles in lukewarm soapy water and dry with a cotton cloth, then polish vigorously with a chamois leather.

Wash filigree gold in lukewarm water with a little *ammonia added, then dry and polish with a leather.

To clean gold and silver lace, sew the lace in a linen cloth. Place the bag in a pan of soapy water (1 pt (0.57 litres) of water to 2 oz (57 grams) soap) and boil for thirty minutes. Rinse thoroughly, still in the bag and then lay the lace out flat to dry.

Enamel Scrub enamelware with soda and hot water, then rinse and dry. If stained, rub with lemon juice and salt, then rinse and dry.

Iron and Steel If the article is in good condition, gently rub with fine emery paper and wipe with a soft cloth dipped in olive oil.

A wire brush can be used on unimportant pieces.

If the article is rusty, soak in *paraffin for one or two days to soften the rust, then gently rub the surface while wet, with emery paper.

If the rust is very bad, flake it off with an old knife or chisel, then soak in *paraffin and brush briskly with a wire brush. When clean, rub with emery powder.

In all cases, when clean, dry thoroughly and seal the surface from the air with vaseline or a mineral oil.

Pewter Mix a thick paste made of cigar ash or whiting and linseed oil. Wet a flannel in a mixture of equal parts of linseed oil and *turpentine, and use this to apply the paste to the article. When clean, wash in hot soapy water, dry thoroughly and polish with a leather.

Silver Polishes Dissolve 1 oz (28 grams) of powdered alum and 4 oz (113 grams) of talcum powder in ½ pt (0.28 litres) of cold water. When thoroughly mixed add four tablespoons of *ammonia and four tablespoons of *turpentine then shake the mixture well. Bottle and keep well corked. Shake before use.

Or, make a paste of French chalk and *methylated spirit, or water mixed with a few drops of *ammonia. Apply the paste to the silver as usual and rub clean with a soft cloth.

Silver Polishing Cloths
Mix ½ pt (0.28 litres) of water to the silver paste and soak towelling rags in the mixture. When saturated hang the cloths up to dry without squeezing. Use these cloths to dry silver after washing.

Silver Dip
Half fill a two pound jam jar with silver paper (chocolate wrappings are the most effective), then add two tablespoons of cooking salt, and fill the jar with cold water. Cover the jar carefully and keep it near the kitchen sink. Dip stained cutlery in the mixture and leave for two minutes to remove the stains, then rinse thoroughly.

Silver Jewelry
Rub the article with toothpaste or damp toothpowder with a soft cloth. Rinse well in warm water and polish with a leather.

Egg Stained Silver
Rub salt on to egg stained silver with the fingertips, then rinse well and clean as usual.

Stainless Steel
Rub stains with a paste made of chalk and water, then wash in hot soapy water; rinse well and dry.
Do not use chemical cleaners or silver polish.

Zinc
To clean zinc, rub with a mixture of salt and white vinegar, or half a lemon dipped in salt. Rinse well and dry thoroughly and polish with a soft cloth.

Leather Wear and Tear To prevent wear and tear and to make old leather supple, rub with any of the following: vaseline, lanolin, castor oil or olive oil. Do not use *paraffin or linseed oil. The oils sink into the leather more easily if warmed. Repeat this application frequently, then polish with a soft cloth. If the leather is very old and hard, apply the oil and then rub with a rag dipped in *turpentine.

Powdery Leather Paint powdery leather with a mixture of castor oil and an alcohol (e.g. *methylated spirit) in a 60-40 volume mixture, and leave for twenty four hours. Then apply pure castor oil to make the leather supple.

Leather Dressing Mix two parts of boiled linseed oil with one part white vinegar in a bottle. Keep tightly corked and shake well before use. Use only a little on a soft cloth and rub well into the leather, then polish with a soft clean duster. Very good for constant use on upholstery and other leather goods in good condition. See below for leather upholstery.

Ingrained Dirt Rub the article with a damp cloth and saddle soap and work up a lather, then wipe off the soap and allow the leather to dry slowly and thoroughly. Then polish with furniture cream (see page 21).

Saddle soap is not a polish, only a cleaner.

Always use a cream polish after using the soap to make the leather supple. The leather will crack if the soap is used on its own.

Leather Upholstery Polish leather upholstery with leather dressing.

Polish smooth and rough grain leathers with furniture polish.

34

occo Leather	Varnish with egg white to restore the lustre.
ok Bindings	See Leather Book Bindings in Paper section (page 40).
ishing Hint	It is important not to use excess polish, to prevent permanent staining. When using liquid dressing, immerse a clean rag in the dressing and wring out the excess liquid before use.
tent Leather	Remove any dust or mud when dry with a very soft brush, then rub the whole surface with vaseline and polish with a clean cloth. To remove fingermarks, rub the surface with cold milk, then dry and polish with a soft cloth.
Suede	Dip a clean flannel in ground oatmeal and rub in a circular motion into greasy stains, then brush out all the powder gently with a wire brush. Repeat the process if necessary. This will not harm the suede. Or, brush greasy stains with lemon juice and a wire brush, then hold in the steam of a boiling kettle for a few minutes and brush dry with a wire brush. In all cases, test an unimportant area first and if in any doubt seek expert advice. Smear very shabby suede with plenty of boot polish and brush into the whole surface very hard. Repeat this several times over a period of days. This will moisten the skin and give the article the appearance of soft kid leather. Polish to a sheen with a soft cloth.
Household Chamois Leathers	Soak the dirty leathers in 1 qt (1.14 litres) of warm water and add a small piece of washing soda and leave for an hour. Wash and rinse in warm water, then gently wring out the excess water and hang up to dry, occasionally pulling and rubbing it into shape.

Drying Shoes

Always dry leather slowly and thoroughly, away from direct heat. Stuff the article with crumpled newspaper to keep its shape and leave to dry in an airy place. The leather must always be completely dry before polishing or oiling.

Boot Cream

Shred 1 oz (28 grams) of white candle wax into an old pan and place it into another pan filled with water. Bring it to the boil until the wax melts. Add four tablespoons of *turpentine and mix together thoroughly.

Shred ½ oz (14 grams) of castile soap or pure soap flakes and mix into a thick paste with a ¼ pt (0.14 litres) of boiling water. Cool the mixtures and mix them together while still liquid, and beat hard into a cream. Add soot to the cream for black shoes. Store the cream in jars.

Waterproofing

Stand the leather soles in boiled linseed oil until they are saturated, then drain and leave to dry. Rub the uppers with castor oil.

A cheap and easy method is to varnish the soles and allow the varnish to dry slowly.

Or, melt together one part mutton fat with two parts beeswax and rub the uppers and stitching thoroughly with the mixture. Leave it to soak in for twelve hours, then rub the surface with a soft cloth. The leather will not polish well for the first few applications of boot polish, but will eventually polish up to a brilliant sheen.

Black and Brown Shoes

Rub black shoes with the inside of the rind of a fresh orange, then polish as usual. Rub brown shoes with the inside of a banana skin, then polish as usual.

These methods act as good restorers.

Creaking Shoes Soak the soles in salt water, then dry slowly and thoroughly. Leave for twelve hours in boiled linseed oil, then drain and dry. This will stop the soles from creaking.

Stains Always deal with stains as soon as possible.

Grease To remove grease stains from leather, rub the stain with a thick paste made of fuller's earth and water. Leave to dry and brush off the powder. Repeat the process if necessary, then polish as usual. This is harmless to the leather and will not remove the colour.

Ink To remove ink stains, cover the stain with damp bicarbonate of soda and change the powder as it discolours until the stain has gone. Then dry well and polish as usual.

Mildew Rub mildew stains with vaseline, then polish as usual.

Rainwater Rub sea water stains with a mixture of one spirit, then polish as usual.

Sea Water Rub sea water stains with a mixture of one teacup of hot milk mixed with a small piece of washing soda, dry slowly and repeat if necessary. If the stain has turned black, mix equal parts of *ammonia and milk and rub the stain gently, then dry slowly and thoroughly. If the leather is hard after drying, rub with castor oil then polish as usual.

PAPER

The Real Copy...

ARGENTINA

SPRAY GLUE

ANTIGA

Furniture

Cake.

Envelopes   Envelopes sealed with egg whites cannot be steamed open.

Parchment and Vellum   Sponge the surface very gently with *lighter petrol to remove grease marks and spots. This will not harm the material, but if in doubt test on an unimportant area or seek expert advice.

Photographs   To clean old photographs, rub gently with stale bread.

Playing Cards   Rub the surface with a soft cloth dipped in a weak solution of camphor oil and warm water.

Prints and Mounting Cards   Always ask a framer to mount prints, drawings and water colours on Museum board which is made of rags and prevents the build up of acids which cause foxing and deterioration. Wood pulp boards allow the build up of acids.

Books   To remove greasy fingermarks from cloth book covers, rub with stale bread or a soft India rubber.

To remove greasy marks from printed music sheets and paper, make a thick paste of fuller's earth and a little water. Spread the mixture thickly over the stain with a knife blade and leave for several hours to dry thoroughly, then brush the powder off.

To remove ink stains gently, dampen with warm water using a soft haired paint brush. Blot up excess inky water. Then wet the stain again with a 5% solution of *oxalic acid. Paint with warm water and dry with white blotting paper, then air well and press gently. If in doubt seek expert advice

Leather Book Bindings

To restore leather bound books, it is best to use The British Museum's Leather Dressing, which is made up of 7 oz (198 grams) anhydrous lanolin 1 oz (28 grams) of cedarwood oil, ½ oz (14 grams) of beeswax and 11 oz (312 grams) of *hexane (or *petroleum ether B.P. 60°-80°).

Use the dressing very sparingly to avoid permanent staining and to prevent books from sticking to each other, when stored.

Immerse a clean cloth in the dressing and wring out all the excess liquid. What remains will be sufficient for the treatment.

After treating with the dressing, leave the book to dry thoroughly for several days. This will protect the hinges, prevent major cracking and make the leather more supple.

The mixture is highly inflammable, so due care must be taken during and after use.

If in any doubt seek advice or see The British Museum's Handbook on Leather Bookbindings by Dr. H. J. Plenderleith.

The dressing is available made up, from Messrs. Hopkins and William Ltd., Freshwater Road, Chadwell Heath, Essex.

Wallpaper

To remove grease spots on wallpaper, place a piece of clean blotting paper over the mark and press with a warm iron. Repeat until the spot has gone.

To strip wallpaper, wet the paper with warm water mixed with a little washing up liquid and let the solution soak in, then gently peel the paper off the wall. This works as well as bought stripper.

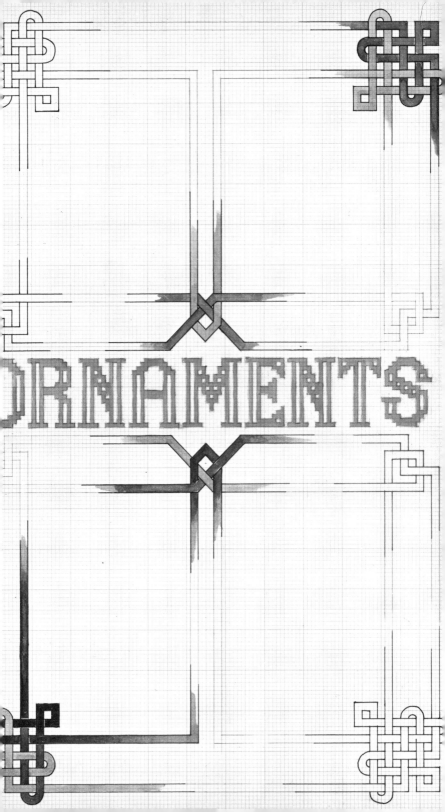

ORNAMENTS

Alabaster *Petrol, *paraffin, *lighter petrol and *nail varnish remover are all safe to use as stain removers. Apply with a soft cloth and rub the stain gently.

*Chloroform will remove beeswax.

Never use water on alabaster.

Amber Wash the article in warm milk or soap and water. Dry and polish with a soft cloth.

Beaded Fabrics Squeeze the article in a basin of *high octane petrol until it is clean. Rinse in fresh petrol and dry outside to remove the smell.

Coral Wash the article in a basin of warm soapy water and polish with tissue paper. If very dirty, boil the article carefully in soapy water with a little washing soda.

Ebony Wipe the article with a damp cloth, then cover with linseed oil and polish with a soft cloth.

Ivory and Piano Keys To clean and polish ivory, rub gently in the direction of the grain, with a fine abrasive paste. Both *lighter petrol or *petrol mixed with finely powdered French chalk, or lemon juice and whiting are suitable. Apply the paste with a damp leather and leave to dry. Then gently brush the powder off and polish with a soft cloth.

Never use water on ivory and where possible leave exposed to sunlight as it yellows in the dark.

Japan Wipe the article with warm water and soap, then dry and dredge in dry flour, leave for one hour then dust and polish with a soft cloth.

Jet To clean carved jet, rub the article with finely ground breadcrumbs. Then polish with a soft cloth.

To clean jet beads, rub with warm olive oil then polish with a soft cloth.

Lacquer To restore the gloss to dull lacquered articles, dip them in warm water with lemon juice or sour milk, then rub with a soft cloth. Dry in a warm place and polish with a leather.

If very dirty, apply a paste made of flour and olive oil rub in well with a cloth, then wipe off and polish with a silk rag.

Marble To clean marble, wash with good quality soap and water using a brush. For less important pieces add a little *ammonia to the water. Dry well and polish.

To polish marble rub the surface with powdered chalk moistened with water. Or sieve two parts washing soda, one part powdered pumice stone and one part powdered chalk and mix into a paste with water. Rub into the marble and leave for twenty four hours. Then wash off with soapy water, dry and polish with a soft cloth.

Unlike alabaster, marble will not be harmed by water, but acids dissolve marble and should be used with great care.

Rust stains can be removed with a 5% solution of *oxalic acid or lemon juice. Then polish as usual. Oil stains can be removed by applying a paste made of powdered kaolin and *petrol. Cover the stain and leave to dry, then wipe off and polish with a soft cloth. *Lighter petrol, *petrol, *alcohol and *nail varnish remover are all safe stain removers.

*Chloroform will remove beeswax.

Ormolu
To clean ormolu scrub with soapy water and a little *ammonia. Rinse well in clean water and dry thoroughly.

To remove lacquer from ormolu rub with a solvent like *methylated spirits.

Papier Mâche
Sponge all papier mâché articles with cold water without soap, then dredge in flour while still damp. When dry, polish with a soft cloth.

Never use hot water, as it will crack the varnish.

Pearls
Never wash artificial pearls. Just rub them with tissue paper to give them an extra sheen.

Wash real pearls in very salty water. Then polish them with a velvet cloth. If in doubt seek expert advice.

Plaster Statuettes
To remove dirt and grease, mix a paste of finely powdered starch and hot water. Apply the paste when hot with a brush to the plaster. Leave to dry, when dry the starch will split and flake off. The grease and dirt will be absorbed by the starch.

Tortoise Shell and Horn
Rub articles with vaseline, olive oil or linseed oil by hand. Then polish off excess oil with a soft cloth. Horn can be rubbed with a damp cloth before oiling.

Mirrors, Windows and Picture Glass

To clean the glass, rub gently with a soft rag dipped in *turpentine, *methylated spirit or *paraffin. Then polish with crumpled newspaper to give a brilliant sheen.

To prevent glass from steaming up, wipe with a soft cloth and a little glycerine, after cleaning and drying.

To make windows opaque temporarily, dissolve two tablespoons of Epsom Salts in 1 pt (0.57 litres) of water and apply the mixture evenly with a sponge.

To remove fly stains from glass, wipe with a woollen cloth dipped in *methylated spirit.

To remove dried paint from windows, rub the paint with the edge of a coin. When all the paint has been scraped away, wipe the window with a damp cloth and polish with a leather. To remove paint spots from glass, rub vigorously with any of the following: linseed oil, hot white vinegar, *turpentine or a strong solution of washing soda.

Glassware

When washing valuable pieces of glass, place a thick towel in the bottom of the washing bowl.

When cut glass clouds and ordinary washing does not clean it, cover the glass with wet potato peelings and leave for twenty four hours. Then rinse in cold water, dry and polish.

Crystal

Cover the shelves used for storing crystal with felt or thick paper, to prevent the glass from chipping or cracking.

Vacuum Flasks

Fill the flask three quarters full of warm water and add half teaspoon of bicarbonate of soda. Replace the stopper and shake vigorously, then rinse well and dry. This will remove the musty smell.

Decanters   To clean decanters, fill with warm water and add one tablespoon of baking powder and crushed eggshells. Leave for twelve hours, stirring occasionally. Then rinse with warm water and a little *ammonia.

To remove wine stains from decanters, pour about two inches of white vinegar into the decanter and add one teaspoon of scouring powder, then fill the decanter with fairly hot water. Shake it vigorously and leave to soak overnight, then shake again, rinse well and wash in hot soapy water. Rinse again and dry.

Bottles   To clean oily bottles, fill them with fine ashes and place in a pan of cold water. Gradually heat the water till it boils then simmer for thirty minutes. When cool, wash out the ashes with cold running water, wash in hot soapy water, then rinse and dry.

Annealing Glass   Immerse the glass in a pan of cold water, then slowly heat until it is boiling. Remove the pan from the heat and leave to cool. This will protect the glass from cracking in very hot water, but if the glass is to be exposed to higher temperatures, boil in oil instead of water.

KITCHEN
THINGS

Aluminium Saucepans Fill burnt aluminium pans with cold water, add two tablespoons of bicarbonate of soda and slowly bring to the boil. Simmer for fifteen minutes. The burnt food will rub off easily. If the stains are very stubborn, repeat the process and simmer for a longer time.

Never use washing soda.

If stained, cook rhubarb or apple peel in the pan.

Cake Tins and Steel Pans Cover new cake tins, baking trays and steel pans with a layer of lard and place in a hot oven until the grease melts and soaks into the surface. Remove from the oven and cool, then wash in warm soapy water and dry thoroughly. This will season the metal and prevent rusting and sticking.

Carbon Steel Knives Wipe the blade clean with a hot damp cloth, and dry immediately. Rub with grease if the knife is not in constant use.

Sharpen with a steel, a stone or an electric knife sharpener.

Remove stains and rust marks by rubbing the blade with a damp piece of very fine emery paper followed by onion juice. Rinse well and dry thoroughly.

Dustbins Burn straw or newspaper in galvanized dustbins to remove any grease or dampness.

Enamel Pans To clean white enamel pans rub the surface with bicarbonate of soda and wash in hot soapsuds. Rinse well and dry thoroughly.

To prevent enamelled pans from burning and discolouring, place an asbestos mat over the cooker ring during heating.

Gummed Labels
Rub the labels with *acetone to remove the gum.

Kettles
To defur, dissolve two teaspoons of borax in the kettle full of water and boil for fifteen minutes, topping up the water if necessary, then rinse well.

Cut off a small piece of loofah and place inside the kettle to collect up the deposits during use. When encrusted, remove the loofah and rinse it well. Save the sediment to clean any enamel goods and replace the loofah inside the kettle.

A marble kept inside the kettle will prevent the furring deposits from sticking to the sides.

Knife Handles
Never immerse knife handles in the washing water, as it loosens the blades and discolours the wood or bone.

Pan Lids
If the knob comes off a pan lid, insert a screw through the hole from the back of the lid and twist on a wine cork.

Refrigerators
Never clean refrigerators with disinfectant, as it will make the food taste of it, and leave a strong smell. Wash the inside with warm water with a teaspoon of bicarbonate of soda, then rinse well with clean water and dry.

Salt Cellars
Smear the salt spots on plated salt cellars with olive oil and leave for several days, then clean as usual.

Teapots
Rub the inside of musty smelling teapots with salt and vinegar, then rinse thoroughly with plenty of warm water.

Scouring Pads   Cut a loofah lengthwise, then cut each half into six. These are much gentler to the hands than wire wool and will not rust.

Collect nylon net fruit bags and put several inside one of the bags and close the end with a piece of string.

Storage Containers   Fill storage jars or plastic containers with tepid water, add a few drops of vanilla essence and leave to soak for forty eight hours. Rinse well and dry thoroughly. This will remove any musty smells.

Soften Hard Water For the best washing results use soft water.

Hard water is softened by adding an alkali. Two to three tablespoons per gallon (4.5 litres) is an approximate guide depending on the hardness of the water. Washing soda, *ammonia or borax are all effective.

Or, add 4 oz (113 grams) of bicarbonate of potash, 4 oz (113 grams) of rose water, 2 oz (57 grams) of pure brandy and 2 oz (57 grams) of lemon juice to 2 qts (2.3 litres) of water. Mix together and store in well corked bottles. When washing, add two tablespoons of the mixture to a gallon (4.5 litres) of water to soften it.

Soaps Soap and water is the only cleaning agent that is equally effective in dealing with sugary, sticky and greasy substances.

Soap Jelly or Soft Soap Used for washing silks, satins, lace and coloured woollens.

Collect all old ends of soaps and shred into a pan. Cover with boiling water and leave to dissolve, then stir well.

The mixture should be allowed to cool until it is thick enough to be lifted in the hands, so more soap or water may need to be added to obtain the right consistency. Make the soap the day before use, to allow it to set.

Honey Soap Shred 2 lbs (0.9 kilograms) of yellow soap into a double saucepan and melt. Add 4 oz (113 grams) of palm oil, 4 oz (113 grams) of honey and a few drops of cinnamon oil. Bring to the boil and simmer for six to eight minutes, then pour into moulds and allow to set. It will be ready for use the following day and is a very superior soap for washing clothes and yourself.

Household Soap	Collect 4 lbs (1.8 kilograms) of waste animal fats and clarify well, then melt the clear fat in a large iron pan. Dissolve 6 oz (170 grams) of *caustic soda into 2 pts (1.14 litres) of water. Follow the instructions on the tin carefully and always add *caustic soda to water. Then very carefully add the dissolved *caustic soda to the warm fat and stir well, taking care not to splash it.

Leave the mixture for twenty four hours until it thickens, stirring it occasionally. Remelt the soap and add 2 pts (1.14 litres) of water and one dessert spoon of coconut oil, then bring to the boil. When fully mixed, divide the contents as follows:

Plain Household Soap	Pour 2½ lbs (1.15 kilograms) of the above mixture into a straight sided wooden box lined with a wet cloth, and leave to set. Then cut into squares and allow to dry thoroughly before use. It can be coloured and scented if desired.
Carbolic Soap	Add ¼ oz (14 grams) of carbolic to 2½ lbs (1.15 kilograms) of the above mixture and stir well and pour into moulds as above. This is a good disinfectant soap.
Sand Soap	Add 3 lbs (1.36 kilograms) of silver sand to 4 lbs (1.8 kilograms) of the above mixture and pour into moulds as above. This is an abrasive scouring soap suitable for floors and stone steps.
Bleaching Liquid	Dissolve one tablespoon of borax in 1 qt (1.14 litres) of boiling water, then add 1 qt (1.14 litres) of cold water. Dip the stained fabric into the solution and dry in the sun. Repeat the process until the stain has disappeared, then rinse the article well in clean water. Test first.

Bleaching   Do not use on wool, silk, leather, resin coated cotton, linen or rayon fabrics that are already weak.

Always test on an unimportant area of fabric before using.

To bleach untreated white cotton, linen and some synthetics, add a cupful of bleach to 1 gallon (4.5 litres) of cold water and mix thoroughly. Soak the article for no longer than thirty minutes, then rinse very thoroughly.

To make a mild solution to remove stains from washable materials, add two tablespoons of bleach to 1 qt (1.14 litres) of cold water and apply it with a medicine dropper, or soak the article in the solution for fifteen minutes. In both cases rinse out the bleach thoroughly. Repeat the process if necessary.

Mix one teaspoon of bleach in a cup of cold water to remove stains from non-washable fabrics. Apply with a dropper and leave for fifteen minutes, then sponge thoroughly with plenty of water.

To make a strong solution for stubborn stains, mix equal parts of bleach and water and apply with a dropper. Rinse immediately with plenty of water and repeat if necessary.

To remove stains in washable fabrics, dissolve two tablespoons of sodium perborate in 1 pt (0.57 litres) of hot water and soak the article for twelve hours. Then rinse out thoroughly. Use lukewarm water for silks and wool.

Apply the above solution with a medicine dropper to the stain on non-washable fabrics and keep the stain damp for several hours until it disappears, then sponge thoroughly with plenty of water.

See pages 87-88 in the Glossary.

Branwater   Tie one breakfast cupful of bran in a piece of cotton and place in a pan with 2 pts (1.14 litres) of water, and bring to the boil. Simmer for half an hour and strain. Add 1 pt (0.57 litres) of luke warm water to the solution and stir well. This is good for washing fine blouses and gaily coloured fabrics, and no soap is needed.

Dilute the mixture to rinse articles in. Do not starch the fabrics as the bran acts as a stiffener when the material is ironed.

Starching   Starching helps to prevent fabrics from getting badly soiled. All natural starches are insoluble in cold water and can only be dissolved by soaking in boiling water.

Gum Arabic Starch   Dissolve 2 oz (57 grams) of white gum arabic powder in 1 pt (0.57 litres) of boiling water, then cover and leave for twelve hours. Then pour the solution into clean bottles, leaving the dregs behind. Add one tablespoon of the mixture to 1 pt (0.57 litres) of starch when ironing cotton, lawn and lace.

Dilute the solution with water for stiffening white muslin.

Scorch Mixture   Peel, slice and pound one large onion and mix it with ½ pt (0.28 litres) of white vinegar, 2 oz (57 grams) of washing soda and 2 oz (57 grams) of fuller's earth, and boil for ten minutes. Then strain the mixture and store in well corked bottles. Spread a little of the mixture on the scorch mark and leave to dry. Repeat the process until the mark has gone.

Colours from Running   Add one teaspoon of Epsom salts to each gallon (4.5 litres) of water used for washing and rinsing.

Setting New Colours Soak the new articles for several hours in the following:

Blue fabrics: add one breakfast cupful of white vinegar to 1 gallon (4.5 litres) of water.

Brown, grey and pink fabrics: add one breakfast cup of salt and teaspoon of alum to 1 gallon (4.5 litres) of water.

Green fabrics: add 4 oz (113 grams) of alum to 3 gallons (13.6 litres) of water.

Checked and patterned fabrics: add half a cup of white vinegar, one cup of salt and one tablespoon of alum to 1 gallon (4.5 litres) of water.

After soaking, hang the fabric in the shade to dry, without wringing, then wash in the usual way.

Waterproofing Melt 1 oz (28 grams) of white wax in 1 qt (1.14 litres) of *turpentine in a double saucepan. When cool dip the fabric into the solution and hang up to dry outside.

Fireproofing Dissolve 2 oz (57 grams) alum in 1 gallon (4.5 litres) of water and dip the fabric in the solution and dry.

Invisible Mending To make an invisible mend, sew with a long human hair instead of cotton. Particularly effective on tweed.

Stitchless Mending Place the damaged area of the fabric on a flat surface, wrong side up. Spread the area with egg white and cover the tear with a piece of fine linen slightly larger than the rip, and press with a hot iron to make the egg stick. This will be almost invisible if done before fraying starts.

FABRICS

HW   1980

Black Cloth To remove the sheen from black cloth, rub the area with a sponge dipped in *turpentine and air well, outside.

Chiffon Wash the article in lukewarm soapy water. Squeeze gently until clean, do not rub, then rinse well. Lay the garment flat on a large towel and pull gently into the shape. Place another towel on top and roll up. When almost dry, press with a warm iron.

Chintz Wash the article in lukewarm soapy water and rinse well. Then add two teaspoons of powdered size to ½ pt (0.28 litres) boiling water. Make sure the size is completely dissolved then strain. Dip the garment into the solution and squeeze out the excess. Roll in a towel to dry partially, then press lightly with a warm iron.

Stiff hot starch can be used if size is not available. Follow the instructions on the packet.

Bran water (see page 56) can be used instead of soap to prevent chintz fading.

Never use washing soda to wash chintz.

Cotton Wash white cotton in very hot soapy water. A mild *chlorine bleach can be added to the wash if necessary. Rinse well in clean water and wring or spin dry. Press with a hot iron while still damp. Starch if necessary.

Coloured cottons can be washed together providing the colours are fast. Add salt to the water to prevent the colours running and wash as above.

Never use strong detergents to wash cottons.

Wash drip dry cottons in plenty of hot water. Do not squeeze as this causes creases. When clean hang up and pull the garment into shape and leave to drip dry.

Damask   To clean damask covers, rub warm bran well into the fabric with a clean flannel and keep changing the flannel. When clean brush out all the bran with a soft brush.

Duvets and   Wash feather filled duvets and eiderdowns
Eiderdowns   individually in a washing machine with hot water and soap. Rinse well and tumble dry. When thoroughly dry shake vigorously to fluff up the feathers.

    Never dry clean feather filled duvets.

    Follow the manufacturer's advice for duvets filled with man made fibre.

Ermine   To clean ermine, mix equal parts of powdered magnesia and cornflour together and rub well into the fur and leave overnight. Then shake and brush the fur to remove all the powder. Repeat if necessary.

Furs   To clean dark furs, warm a quantity of bran in a pan, and stir it continuously to prevent it from burning. Rub the warm bran well into the fur by hand, then shake it out.

    Repeat the process until the bran appears clean, then shake and brush the fur to remove all the bran. This method can also be used for Angora rugs.

    To gloss the edges, rub with a cloth dipped in *methylated spirit.

    To clean light coloured furs, first rub in damp warm bran with a dry flannel, until the bran is dry. Then shake the fur well and rub in dry warmed bran with a piece of white muslin, and shake again. Then rub in powdered magnesia against the way of the fur until clean. Shake and brush well to remove all the powders. If in any doubt, consult an expert.

Georgette   Wash in warm pure white soap flakes, and squeeze gently by hand. Lift the article up and down in the water taking care not to strain the fabric. When clean, rinse in warm water and repeat until the water is clear. Gently squeeze out the excess water and roll in a thick towel. Press, when damp, with a warm iron.

Lace   Handle lace with care. Always squeeze the fabric when washing, never rub it.

Wash white lace in pure soap flakes and hot water mixed together to make a thick lather. Pour the soap solution into a jar and add the lace, then cover the jar and shake it for five minutes. Change the soap and repeat the process until the lace is clean. Rinse well in warm then cold water.

Then dissolve one teaspoon of gum starch (see page 56) in 1 pt (0.57 litres) of water and dip the lace into it. Squeeze out the excess water and roll in a thick towel. Lay the lace flat, face down on a damp ironing board and pull it into shape, then pin it. Cover with a damp cloth and press with a cool iron.

To clean fragile lace, immerse in a bowl of *petrol and squeeze gently by hand. Repeat if necessary in fresh petrol until the lace is clean, then dry outside.

To freshen black lace, dissolve a few drops of *ammonia in 1 pt (0.57 litres) of water and gently sponge the lace with the solution until it is damp. Roll the lace in a cloth and leave for half an hour, then press as above.

Never wash black lace.

Store valuable lace in blue tissue paper to preserve its colour.

See gold lace in Metals section, (page 30).

Lambskins To clean lambskins, rub in plenty of powdered magnesia by hand and leave overnight. Then shake and brush until all the powder is removed.

If in any doubt when cleaning furs consult an expert.

Linen White linen sheets, napkins and tablecloths can be washed as white cotton.

Natural coloured linen needs gentler treatment. Wash in cooler water and do not bleach.

Wash dyed linen carefully, squeezing the fabric as little as possible.

Press all linens while damp with a fairly hot iron.

Muslin Add one teaspoon of salt to a bucket of cold water and soak the garment in it for half an hour. Then add a tablespoon of soap jelly (see page 53) to a basin of warm water, and beat into a lather. Wash the article in the solution by kneading and squeezing, then repeat the process in a fresh soap solution until clean. Mix a little white vinegar or starch to warm water and rinse the garment well in it.

Starch slightly and iron when damp with a warm iron. (see page 56.)

Satin Add half a tablespoon of *paraffin to every quart (1.14 litres) of warm soapy water needed to immerse the article. Lift the garment up and down in the mixture until clean. Then rinse several times in clear warm water and add a little borax to the final rinse to restore the gloss. Squeeze out the excess water and partially dry, then press on the wrong side with a warm iron.

Serge   Wash a handful of ivy leaves and place in an old pan, adding 1 qt (1.14 litres) of water. Bring to the boil and simmer for twenty minutes, then strain and store in well corked bottles. Sponge the shiny areas of black and navy serge with the mixture to eliminate the sheen.

Silk   Completely dissolve pure soap flakes in hand hot water and add the garment. Agitate gently and repeat the process with clean suds. Rinse well in warm then cold water. Add one or two tablespoons of gum starch (see page 56) to every gallon (4.5 litres) of water used in the final rinse, to stiffen the silk. Then squeeze out the excess water and roll in a thick towel. Press while damp with a warm iron. Re-wet the silk rather than sprinkle with water if it is too dry to iron, as sprinkled water can mark the fabric.
   Do not stiffen Shantung silk.

Velvet   Add a little *ammonia to a pan of boiling water and hold the velvet pile down over the steam. Then hold the damp fabric over a hot iron to raise the pile and freshen.
   Gently rub grease marks with a cloth dipped in *turpentine until dry. Repeat if necessary. Then brush lightly and hang outside to air.

Viyella   Wash Viyella as for wool (see next page).
   Iron with a fairly hot iron when almost dry, on the right side for light colours and the wrong side for dark colours.

Angora Wool   To prevent Angora wool from shedding, place the garment in a plastic bag and leave in the refrigerator overnight. The effect will last for twenty four hours.

Wool General Rules

Wash woollens in hand hot water. Avoid extremes of temperature or they will shrink.

Do not soak woollens or leave wet.

Do not rub, twist or wring the fabric.

Do not use *ammonia or too much soap and always rinse well.

Do not machine wash unless especially programmed for wool.

Wash wool in hand hot water with pure soap flakes. Dissolve the soap completely before adding the garment. Agitate gently and repeat the process in clean suds. Rinse thoroughly in warm water, and add salt if the colours are likely to run.

Squeeze out excess water or spin dry for a few minutes. Arrange garment on a hanger and pull gently into shape, or lay flat on a thick towel t dry. Cover the dry article with a damp cloth and press with a warm iron if necessary, and air well.

Man Made Fibres Follow the manufacturer's instructions for washing.

STAINS

General Rules   Remove stains as soon as possible.

Consider the composition of fabric as well as the type of stain.

Try the least harmful method first. Always test chemical solvents on an unimportant area of the fabric first.

After using chemicals, rinse the fabric well.

After using bleach, boil the article if possible and dry outside.

After using acids, neutralise the effect with an alkali rinse.

Strong acids and alkalis should only be used in weak solutions mixed with warm water, never boiling water, as they are harmful to certain materials. e.g. Wool and woollen mixtures, silks, nylons, terylene, orlon and all coloured materials.

See pages 82-84 for acids and alkalis.

Do not use nail varnish remover on acetates, rayon or tricel.

Do not use grease solvents, except soap on plastics.

Do not use *oxalic acid on silks or wool.

Acid   To restore the colour to fabrics faded by acid, sponge with a little *ammonia and water, followed by *chloroform.

Beer   Washable fabrics: ordinary washing often removes the stain, but if ineffective, rewash the garment adding a little white vinegar or *ammonia to warm soapy water. Then rinse well and dry.

Unwashable fabrics: sponge the stain with *methylated spirit, then rub a little hard soap into the mark and leave to dry. When dry, brush the fabric well.

Alcohol Washable fabrics: rinse in clear warm water until the stain has gone, then wash as usual. White linen and cotton can be bleached if necessary.

Unwashable fabrics: sponge with clear warm water, and dry well.

Blood Washable fabrics: soak freshly stained fabrics in cold water, then wash with soap and cold water and rinse well. Bleach white fabrics if necessary and soak silks in a borax and water solution of 2 oz to 1 pt (56 grams to 0.57 litres) and rinse well. Then wash all fabrics as usual.

Soak old dried blood stained fabrics in biological washing powder and cold water overnight, or add two cupfuls of salt to 1 gallon (4.5 litres) cold water and soak article for up to twelve hours. Bleach white fabrics after soaking if necessary. Then wash all fabrics as usual.

Unwashable fabrics: sponge the stain with cold water. Then make a paste of starch and cold water and spread it on thickly, leaving it to dry and absorb the stain. When dry, brush off lightly with a soft brush. This is harmless even to delicate fabrics.

Coffee Washable fabrics: sponge fresh stains with the above borax solution. Then rinse, and wash as usual.

Sponge old stains with cold water, then rub well with glycerine. Leave for half an hour and rinse with warm water. Bleach white fabrics if necessary. Then wash all fabrics as usual.

Unwashable fabrics: sponge the fabric with clear warm water or the above borax solution and rub dry. If any stain is left, sponge with a grease solvent (see pages 85-87).

Cocoa and Chocolate Washable fabrics: sponge the stain with cold water. Never use hot water. Then add 1 oz (28 grams) of borax to 1 pt (0.57 litres) of warm water, and sponge the stain with the solution. Then rinse well and wash the article as usual.

Unwashable fabrics: sponge the mark with *carbon tetrachloride, testing the fabric first in an unimportant area. Then sponge again with the above borax solution.

Egg Washable fabrics: soak the fabric in a warm solution of biological washing powder and water. Then wash as usual.

Unwashable fabrics: sponge the stain with the above solution.

Fruit and Fruit Juice Washable fabrics: if the stain is fresh, stretch the fabric over a basin and pour boiling water through the stain from a height. Then wash as usual.

Or, cover the stain with dry starch and leave for one hour, then brush off and wash the garment as usual.

Rub old stains with glycerine and leave for one hour. Pour boiling water through the stain and repeat the process if necessary. Then wash as usual.

Unwashable fabrics: sponge the stain with cold water, then glycerine, and leave for one hour, and rub with a grease solvent (see pages 85-87).

Gravy Wash or sponge with lukewarm detergent suds. Soak old or severe stains in cool salt water mixed with a little *ammonia, then wash in cool suds.

Never wash gravy stains with hot water.

Grass　Washable fabrics: wash in hot suds when possible, or sponge the stain with *methylated spirit, then wash as usual.

Sponge nylons and synthetics with a solution of equal parts warm water and *methylated spirit and rinse well, then wash as usual.

Rub severe stains with glycerine and leave for one hour, then wash as usual.

Unwashable fabrics: sponge the stain with *methylated spirit, eucalyptus oil or *ether, then wipe with a cloth dipped in clean water, and pat dry.

Grease and Oil　Washable fabrics: wash the article in very hot soapless detergent if possible. If not, place a clean cloth or blotting paper under the stain and sponge with *carbon tetrachloride or *petrol. Then wash and rinse thoroughly.

Unwashable fabrics: sponge the fabric on the wrong side with *petrol or *carbon tetrachloride. Test the fabric first to make sure it is not badly affected by the solvents.

Ink　Washable fabrics: soak fresh stains immediately in cold water.

Sponge white fabrics, after soaking, with a 5% solution of *oxalic acid and warm water. Then rinse well and wash as usual.

Dip old stains on white fabrics in cold water, then cover the stain with a paste of cream of tartar and lemon juice and leave for one hour. Rinse throughly and wash as usual.

Sponge coloured fabrics with *petrol or *turpentine, then rinse well and wash in soapless detergent.

Unwashable fabrics: apply the same solutions and recipes as above with a sponge, then pat dry with a dry cloth.

Ballpoint and Felt Tip Pen Inks
Drip *methylated spirit or *carbon tetrachloride onto the stain. First test the solvents on an unimportant area to make sure they do not harm the fabric. When the ink has dissolved, rub with a clean cloth dipped in more of the spirit. Repeat the process with a clean cloth, until the stain has gone.

Iron Mould or Rust
Stretch stained white linen and cotton over a bowl and pour boiling water from a height through the stain. Then cover the mark with a paste of cream of tartar and lemon juice and rinse quickly in water containing a little *ammonia. Repeat if necessary then wash and boil the garment.

Soak coloured fabrics in a little lemon juice or sour milk and leave for two or three minutes. Then rinse thoroughly and wash as usual.

Lipstick
Washable fabrics: scrape off as much as possible with a blunt knife, then wash in hot soapless detergent.

Rub severe stains with glycerine, eucalyptus oil or vaseline before washing.

Unwashable fabrics: sponge with a grease solvent (see pages 85-87).

Mud
Washable fabrics: allow the mud to dry then brush off the excess with a soft brush. Rub the remaining stain with boiled potato water or a weak solution of borax: 1 oz (28 grams) of borax to 1 pt (0.57 litres) of water, then rinse well and wash as usual.

Unwashable fabrics: allow mud to dry and brush off as much as possible. Rub the remaining stain with *carbon tetrachloride. Test the fabric first to make sure it is not harmed by the solvent.

Mildew Wash newly formed stains in hot soapy water as soon as possible, then rinse and dry outside.

    For obstinate stains on white fabrics soak in a solution of one part chlorine bleach to eight parts cold water for about ten minutes. Then wring out the water and place the article in a weak solution of cold water and white vinegar to neutralise the bleaching action. Rinse well and wash as usual.

Milk Washable fabrics: rinse the fabric in cool water, then wash with cold soapless detergent suds.

    Soak stains in delicate fabrics in equal parts of glycerine and warm water and rub gently. When the stain is loose, wash in tepid soapy water, then rinse and dry. Or soak the stain in *methylated spirit for about two minutes, then wash with soap jelly (see page 53).

    Unwashable fabrics: sponge the stain with *methylated spirit, then dab with cold water.

Paints Rub dried gloss paint stains with *trichlorethylene. Test the fabric first and follow the instructions on the bottle carefully.

    Enamel paint: sponge the stains with *turpentine or mix equal parts of *ammonia and *turpentine. Soak the garment until the stain has dissolved, then wash in the usual way in soapy suds.

    Soften dried enamel paint stains with two parts of *ammonia mixed with one part *turpentine or *paraffin and rub into the marks, then wipe clean with a cloth and dry.

    Paint or varnish: sponge new and old stains on delicate fabrics with *ether or *chloroform.

    Emulsion paint: soak or sponge fresh stains with cold water, then wash in the usual way.

Nail Varnish Before attempting to remove the stain with any of the following chemicals, test the fabric first in an unimportant area to avoid damage.

Protect work surfaces, as *acetone will damage paint and varnish.

Washable fabrics: sponge fresh stains with *acetone or *nail varnish remover and wipe with a clean cloth until the stain fades.

Dampen old stains on rayon and tricel with a little *carbon tetrachloride, then drip *amyl acetate on to the softened stain, and wipe with a clean cloth. *Acetone can be used after the carbon tetrachloride except on rayon and tricel. Finally wash with warm soapy water.

Unwashable fabrics: follow the above process, but do not wash. Instead dab the affected area with *methylated spirit and wipe dry with a soft cloth.

Perfume Washable fabrics: wash fresh stains immediately in warm clear water. Rub dry stains with glycerine, then wash as usual.

Unwashable fabrics: rub the stain with glycerine and leave for one hour, then rinse by sponging with clean warm water.

Perspiration Sponge the stains with any of the following: a weak solution of white vinegar and water, or lemon juice; or dissolve two aspirins in water and soak the article; or soak the article in a mild solution of soapless detergent. In all cases, rinse very well, then wash as usual.

Toffee Soak the stained fabric in warm water to dissolve the sugar. Add a few drops of *methylated spirit and a little white vinegar to the water if the stain is very obstinate. Rinse well, then wash as usual.

Tar Scrape off the thick surface tar with a blunt knife, then soften the remaining stain with butter or lard, and rub with *turpentine or *petrol or *paraffin. Do not use water as this makes it spread.

Sponge delicate fabrics with oil of eucalyptus. Then in all cases wash as usual.

Tea Washable fabrics: pour boiling water over stains in white fabrics while still fresh. Bleach if necessary, and add a little vinegar to the final rinse, then wash as usual.
Coloured fabrics: sponge coloured fabrics with a warm borax solution: 1 oz (28 grams) borax to 1 pt (0.57 litres) of water, and rub the stain hard. Rinse thoroughly and wash as usual.

Unwashable fabrics: rub the stain with glycerine and leave for one hour, then sponge with *carbon tetrachloride or *methylated spirit.

Test the fabric first in an unimportant area if using *carbon tetrachloride.

Urine Urine is acid, therefore sponge the stain with a mild *ammonia solution, or bicarbonate of soda and water to neutralise the acid. The stain can then be rinsed out in clean warm water. Wash in the usual way.

Vinegar Mix one teaspoon of *ammonia to 1 pt (0.57 litres) of water and soak or sponge the article, and then leave it for a few minutes. Rinse well and wash as usual.

Wax Place blotting paper over the stain and press with a hot iron. Change the paper until all the grease has been absorbed. Use tissue paper and a cooler iron on silks and delicate fabrics.

Water   Hold water stained articles in the steam of a boiling kettle until the material is damp, and shake frequently, then press with a warm iron. This is often enough to remove the stain.

Dip rayons, silks and delicate fabrics stained by sprinkled water, in warm water. Gently squeeze out the excess water and roll in a towel, then iron while damp.

Rub rainwater spots with *methylated spirit and a clean cloth.

Sea Water   Rub the fabric with white vinegar to restore the colour.

Brush dried stains to remove the salt then soak in warm water until all the salt has dissolved. Rinse and wash as usual. Repeat the process if necessary.

Wine   Washable fabrics: pour boiling water through the stain until it fades, or soak the article in a hot borax solution 1 oz (28 grams) to 1 pt (0.57 litres) of water. Or, rub the stain with lemon juice and salt. In all cases rinse well and wash as usual.

Sponge wool with *hydrogen peroxide solution (20 vol. strength, one part to six parts cold water). Then rinse well and wash as usual.

Unwashable fabrics: sponge the stain with the above borax solution, repeating several times, and rub dry with a clean cloth.

Rub coloured fabrics with warm soap suds or very weak *ammonia solution, then rub dry.

CLEAN AS A WHISTLE
THE
PAPER

ODDS + ENDS

Sponges

Loofahs

Feathers

Furniture

Feathers

Lemons

M

O

M

S

T
F

S
Y
T

Baths　To clean enamel or vitreous china baths, rub the sides with *paraffin and a clean cloth. Then rinse well with hot water.

Brushes　To straighten bent bristles, hold them in the steam of a boiling kettle, then remove from the steam and pull them straight by hand. Repeat if necessary. Steam can cause severe burns, so care must be taken.

Soak new bristle brushes with wooden heads in cold water for about two hours, to swell the wood and secure the bristles. Then dry in a shaded place with the head of the brush off the ground.

Wash all household bristle brushes in hot soapy water with a little washing soda, then plunge them into cold water and dry, head up in the sun.

To clean hair brushes, first remove the hair and dust, then treat the back and handle according to the material. Wash the bristles by beating them up and down in 1qt (1.14 litres) of warm soapy water with one teaspoon of *ammonia added. Rinse in warm, then cold water with a little salt to stiffen the bristles. Then shake well and hang up to dry.

Cork　To clean cork mats, wash in cold water and rub with a smooth pumice stone. Then rinse under cold running water and dry in a cool place.

Curtain　Before use, rub curtain hooks with an oily rag.
Hooks　This prevents rusting and helps to protect the curtains from tearing.

To renovate old hooks, soak them in water with a little *ammonia added. Then rinse in clean water and dry well.

Feathers To clean decorative feathers, soak them in a basin of *high octane petrol until they are clean, then dry outside.

To clean white ostrich feathers, shred 4 oz (113 grams) of white soap and dissolve it in 4 pts (2.27 litres) of hot water in a large basin. Beat the mixture into a lather, and soak the feathers in it, rubbing them gently by hand until they are clean. Then rinse in clean hot water. Shake well and hang up to dry.

To prepare feathers for stuffing cushions, cut off the downy tops and store them in paper bags until there are enough to fill a cushion. Heat the bags in a moderate oven for about half an hour. Check the oven frequently to prevent the bags from catching fire.

Before stuffing the cushion, rub the ticking with beeswax to stop the feathers working through the material.

Keys and Zip Fasteners To make stiff zips and keys work smoothly, rub the teeth with a lead pencil. This will last for months and is a non-greasy lubricant.

Kneeling Pad Fill an old hot water bottle with chopped foam rubber to make a very comfortable kneeling pad.

Pests To catch fleas in beds, remove the bedclothes gently, and once the flea is found, dab it quickly with a piece of wet soap. This slows the flea down and makes it easier to catch.

Clusters of cloves hung up in a room will keep flies away.

To destroy cockroaches, mix equal parts of oatmeal with plaster of Paris and spread on the floor of the infested area. The cockroaches will eat this and later die.

Pin Cushions   Sew a pin cushion cover and fill it with dry coffee grounds. The needles and pins will not rust when stored in it.

Plants   To keep plants watered while away on holiday, stand a bucket of water near the plants. Cut lengths of thick wool and place one end in the water and the other end into the plant pot. The wool will absorb the water which will then drip onto the soil.

Rusty Irons   To clean a rusty iron, tie a piece of beeswax in a rag and rub the iron with the cloth when hot. Then scour the surface with a cloth sprinkled with salt. This will make the iron as clean and smooth as new. Keep the waxed cloth for further use.

Smells   To get rid of the smell of new paint, place a handful of hay into a bucket of warm water and leave in the room overnight.

To prevent the smell of cabbage or cauliflower occurring, add a little lemon juice to the water while cooking.

Add lemon skins to the washing-up water to eliminate the smell of fish and onions from china and cutlery. It also softens the water and makes the china shine.

Sponges and Loofahs   Soak sponges and loofahs when slimy in a strong solution of vinegar and water for twenty four hours. Then rinse several times in cold water and dry outside.

Rusty Screws   To remove rusty screws that have become stuck, cover the head of the screw with *paraffin and leave it to soak in. Add more *paraffin if necessary.

78

Umbrellas When new, grease the hinges well with vaseline to prevent rusting.

To revive old silk umbrellas, dissolve one tablespoon of sugar in ½ pt (0.28 litres) of boiling water. Open the umbrella and sponge the silk with the sugar solution, segment by segment from the shaft out to the tips. Then hang the open umbrella on a line to dry.

GLOSSARY

BEESWAX	CAUSTIC SODA	EPSOM SAL

LINSEED OIL	SOAP	VASELIN

CHLOROFORM	BLEACH	TURPENTI

WHITING	OLIVE OIL	ACETON

LANOLIN	AMMONIA	PARAFFI

OXALIC ACID	SALT	CASTOR O

FULLER'S EARTH	FRENCH CHALK

ENERAL RULES All the ingredients mentioned in this book are available from chemists, hardware stores, builders' merchants or artists' shops. They divide naturally into eight sections according to their functions. Some have several uses and may be found under a number of headings.

Please pay careful attention to the warnings on usage where they are given.

ABRASIVES These are used for polishing or rubbing away other substances.

They vary in hardness and coarseness.

For polishing, use a comparatively coarse grade initially, gradually substituting finer grades.

Some abrasives have additives to aid in cleaning.

Steel Wool Grade 000 is the finest grade of steel wool.

Sandpaper Sandpaper is also available in different grades.

Emery Paper and Powder This is a variety of mineral corundum in fine granular form, available in different grades. It is used for polishing metals, hard stones and for reconditioning furniture and smoothing chips in glass.

Pumice Powder This is a porous volcanic stone containing silica. Many commercial scouring powders contain pumice.

Salt It can be used as an abrasive. (See alkalis)

Whiting This is a very finely powdered chalk used in cleaning powders, polishes and in making putty. It is available from artists' shops or painting and decorating stores.

ABSORBENTS These are used for the removal of light, fresh or greasy stains, by absorbing the staining substance which can then be easily brushed away. They are harmless to all fabrics but it is not recommended to use them on dark unwashable materials. They often work more effectively if made into a paste with water before applying to the stain.

Fuller's Earth This is a hydrated compound of silica and alumina. It is obtainable from a chemist.

French Chalk This is a soapstone or talc. In solid form it is used as tailor's chalk.

Other Absorbents Oatmeal, bran, salt, sand, stale breadcrumbs, talcum powder, starch, blotting paper, soft cloths, cotton wool, paper napkins and tissues are all absorbents.

ACIDS Acids neutralise alkalis and will dissolve in water.

Oxalic Acid This is obtained from the sorrel plant and is sold in crystal form.
Commonly used in 5% solution, always adding the crystals to the water.
Do not use on synthetic fabrics.
*It is poisonous if swallowed. Avoid contact with skin or eyes.

Acetic Acid and Vinegar It can be used as a 10% solution to remove stains, but more often white vinegar is used as it contains 5% acetic acid and is usually strong enough to deal with most stains.

Citric Acid   This is obtained from many fruit juices but especially from lemons. It can be bought from the chemist in diluted or powdered form, but lemon juice is equally as effective.

ALKALIS   Alkalis neutralise acids and are soluble in water.
     *Poisoning and burns from strong alkalis can be treated in an emergency by liberally applying vinegar or citric acid.

Caustic Soda   This is a very strong alkali sold in crystal form.
     *Always add the crystals to the water.
     *Never add any other cleaning agents to caustic soda.
     *It is extremely poisonous and inhaling the vapours should be avoided.
     Avoid any contact with the skin or eyes as it can cause severe burning. If it does splash onto the skin, flood the burn with running water immediately.

Common Salt   It is an excellent cleaner and stain remover.

Ammonia   It is an alkaline gas dissolved in water and can be bought in varying strengths from chemists and hardware stores. 5%-15% solutions are the most suitable. The chemical 10% pure solution is best for stain removal and cleaning.
     *Ammonia is poisonous if swallowed. Store well stoppered in a cool place out of the reach of children.
     *Avoid contact with the skin or eyes.
     *Never mix ammonia with any other cleaning agent as the combination could produce lethal gases.

Cloudy Ammonia This is equally as caustic as ordinary ammonia and must be used with similar care.

It is a useful heavy household cleaner, excellent for scrubbing floors and lavatory cleaning.

To make cloudy ammonia, dissolve 2 oz (57 grams) of borax and 1 oz (28 grams) of powdered, castile soap in one quart of hot water, then add 1 pint of ammonia and ¼ pint (0.14 litres) of *methylated spirit when the solution is cool. Add one or two tablespoons to 1 gallon of water for use.

Washing Sodas An effective cleaner sold in crystal form.

It is very soluble in water and acts as a water softener.

EMULSIFIERS These are substances that mix with grease or resinous particles and hold them in suspension making them easy to remove or dissolve.

Ammonia and washing soda are both emulsifiers (see above).

Soap Soaps are known as built or unbuilt.

Unbuilt soaps contain a high proportion of pure soap with a little moisture and salt. They are expensive and very mild, suitable for toiletries and laundering fine fabrics.

Built soaps contain additives like borax, alkaline water softeners and washing soda, etc., which help in removing heavily soiled cloths. They are very effective in hard water.

Synthetic Detergents They have good wetting and penetrating properties and are more easily rinsed out of fabrics than soap.

SOLVENTS	These are substances which, when applied, mix with and dissolve the material to be removed. There are many types of solvents so it is important to analyse the stain to be removed and select the correct solvent.
Water	Water and steam dissolve water based glues, sugary substances and salts.
Alcohol	It absorbs water freely and is useful for drying wet fragile articles by absorbing the water and then evaporating.
Methylated Spirit or Wood Spirit	*This is poisonous, highly inflammable with a strong noxious vapour. Care must be taken during use. Only use in a well ventilated space, away from any naked flames. Store well stoppered in a cool place out of reach of children. It is safe to use on most fabrics and evaporates quickly.
Surgical Spirit	This is a powerful disinfectant. It is much weaker than methylated spirit.
Ethyl Alcohol	This is the main alcoholic content of wines, beers and spirits. Gin is useful for cleaning certain stones in jewelry.
Acetone	*This is a highly inflammable colourless liquid, with a heavy toxic peppermint smell. Avoid breathing the fumes or contact with the eyes. Only use in a well ventilated place. Do not use near naked flames. Store well-stoppered in a cool place, out of reach of children. It is harmless to natural fibres but will damage synthetic materials, including acetates. Paraffin will counteract the action of acetone.

Amyl Acetate *This is a chemical compound of acetic acid and amyl alcohol with a heavy toxic smell of peardrops. Avoid breathing the vapour or contact with eyes, and always use in a well ventilated place. It is also highly inflammable, so avoid using near naked flames. It is also poisonous if taken internally.

Ethyl Acetate *This acts in a similar way to amyl acetate, and has the same heavy toxic fumes and is highly inflammable.

Carbon Tetrachloride *This is a clear non-inflammable liquid which evaporates very rapidly, giving off a heavy toxic vapour. Avoid breathing the fumes and contact with the eyes. Always use in a well ventilated place.

Trichlor-ethylene *Similar to carbon tetrachloride but less toxic. Follow the above precautions carefully.

Chloroform *This is a colourless liquid with a powerful toxic vapour. It evaporates very rapidly and the fumes have a strong anaesthetic effect if breathed. Always use in a well ventilated place and avoid breathing the vapour or contact with the eyes.

Petrol Lighter Fuel *This is a super-refined petrol with all the properties of ordinary petrol, so the same precautions apply.

Paraffin *This is obtained by distilling crude petroleum and is highly inflammable and must not be used near a naked flame.

Petrol   *This is a spirit distilled from petroleum, which evaporates at normal temperatures. In liquid form it is highly inflammable but if confined in a container with air it will explode violently when in contact with fire. Use with great care, well away from naked flames. Avoid breathing the fumes or contact with the eyes, and use in a well ventilated place.

Never use it to clean silk as the rubbing friction can cause a spark which could explode the vapour.

Turpentine   *This is a resinous juice obtained from pine and fir trees and is highly inflammable and poisonous. Avoid using near naked flames and breathing the vapour. Always use in a well ventilated place.

White Spirit   *This is the commercially produced substitute for turpentine and is highly inflammable.

It does not contain any of the natural oils found in turpentine, so should not be used in making polishes.

BLEACHES   Bleaches are chemical agents used to whiten materials, especially white fabrics, and to remove certain stains.

Always follow the instructions on the container and use with care.

*They weaken fabrics and fade colours if not used properly.

*Do not store in metal containers.

Citric Acid and Vinegar   Both these have mild bleaching powers.

Chlorine Bleach This is ordinary household bleach.
    *Do not use on wool, silk, leather or resin-coated cotton, linen and rayon fabrics that are already weak.
    Always test on an unimportant area of fabric before using, and rinse very throroughly after use.
    Do not add bleach to water containing clothes.
    *Never mix chlorine bleach with any other cleaning agents like ammonia, etc., as they mix to give off dangerous toxic fumes.

Sodium Perborate Bleach This is not as strong as chlorine bleach and is safe to use on all fabrics.
    It is obtainable from the chemist in crystal form.
    *Do not store in metal containers.

Hydrogen Peroxide This is a good bleach, safe to use on all fabrics. It is available from the chemist as 20 vol. strength and is used diluted; 1 part to 6 parts cold water.
    *Always pour down the drain once used, and store in a cool dark place away from children.

OILS These lubricate dried leather and soften certain stains to make removal easier.

Lanolin This is obtained from the natural grease of wool. It is a lubricant.

Castor Oil It is obtained from the bean of the castor oil plant. It is a good leather conditioner and is particularly effective on leathers that need to be polished.

Linseed Oil	This originates from the flax plant, used for making varnishes, paints and many furniture polishes.
	When buying, specify whether 'raw' or 'boiled' linseed oil is wanted.
	For recipes which recommend boiled linseed oil, this does not mean that it is necessary to boil the oil, but is a special process that can be done only by experts.
Vaseline or ʳoleum Jelly	It is a soft greasy substance obtained from petroleum.